Zen Bud _ın for Beginners

A Simple and Easy Buddhism Guide to Finding Your Inner Peace and Happiness

Table of Contents:

Introduction

This book contains proven steps and strategies on how to incorporate the basic elements of Zen Buddhism into your life and reap the benefits that are bound to follow. Through Zen, you will be able to let go of those thoughts that are plaguing you, and reach a complete and utter peace of mind.

Because the principles of Zen Buddhism affect the mind the personal intellect can have a hard time grasping its concept. Therefore, the following pages of this book are meant for informational purposes, not as instructions. This book attempts to provide: the tools necessary to begin the study of the mind, and with the help of Zazen, see into one's own nature.

Many people will tell you that it is just a matter of sitting without goals, but the truth is far from it. This so called 'sitting' is an entire journey of self-discovery, of an intimate, spiritual self-development. During which time you train your mind to focus better and unveil your life's purpose.

Zen Buddhism invites you to transform yourself spiritually and live in harmony with the world and the people around you. While many other religions can say the same, Zen Buddhism always strives for the purification of the mind. It urges you to face yourself, to face everything you like and dislike about who you are and what you do.

Buddhism also challenges you to change the fundamental precepts of the life you have been taught so far, regarding materialism, ambition, pride, greed and revenge. Rather, it pushes you towards a general goodness of being. Wisdom, empathy, charity, tolerance and discipline are encouraged to grow.

The results of this spiritual cultivation are numerous. Most importantly, you will begin a journey that all humans strive for in this world: the attainment of a meaningful and joyful life, where you are focused and aware of every single moment.

Thanks again for downloading this book, I hope you enjoy it!

Chapter 1: What Is Zen Buddhism?

Let me start by saying that defining the term 'Zen Buddhism' and how it affects people's lives is a tricky endeavor. Not because it is this super complicated practice, theory or dogma, but rather because it affects all people differently. Like any practical experience, it is simply not enough just to explain an idea to someone and expect that person to know exactly what it is without ever having tried it.

It's like one of those situations where a person is trying out a new dish for the first time. You can go out of your way to explain it. You can tell how all the blends of flavors and the ingredients work together to create a unique taste. You can describe the unique texture of the food.

But it's impossible for you to explain the overall effect that this unity has. You cannot say how it will transfer onto that person's palate. As is the case with many things in life, the best way to understand something is to simply try it out for your-self.

This book will provide the reader with a general perspective on what Zen Buddhism incorporates. What kind of a practice it is and how it can help you lead a healthier, stress-free life-style. Simply by learning how to let go of those things that present an unnecessary burden you can achieve your goals.

Zen Buddhism originated around 2500 years ago. Then referred to as the spiritual awakening of a man whose name was Siddhartha Gautama, also known as The Buddha. Zen, in this combination of words and practices, refers to Zen meditation or Zazen, which is usually done in a seated position.

During this practice, one endeavors to reach higher levels of self-discovery and psychological vigilance. It is something that many people in the modern world are unable to obtain. Due to the hectic nature of their everyday lives, many people have lost the ability to look inside themselves.

It is not a question of intellectually understanding or grasping what Zen Buddhism is, because it is not a simple piece of knowledge or a theory. Not that one learns by heart and then transfers onto their students. It is not a religion that tells you what you should and shouldn't believe in.

On the contrary, Zen Buddhism teaches one how to think, with a special focus on when not to do so. Zen meditation requires a lack of thought to be able to fully open up for a spiritual awakening. Once a person is able to totally clear the mind, the state that is achieved is a vastly open space of spiritual wonder.

There is no set rule to follow or guidelines to go by to say what you can or cannot accomplish in this state. The only thing required is to open your mind to the possibilities of what the mind has to offer. It focuses on the current moment and it endorses the old adage of Carpe Diem, in other words, it urges us to seize the day.

This is simply saying that we should live in the present, not the past or the future. It teaches us not to live in the past, because it is done and gone, and we can't bring it back. Dwelling on it doesn't do us any good. Reliving our mistakes in our mind and wishing we'd done differently will never make it so, and therefore, is a waste of effort.

Rather, Zen Buddhism teaches you to have a different perspective on your past: to embrace what you've done well, but also what you've done wrong. No mistake is futile if you manage to extract a valuable lesson out of it. One must understand that all things are universally connected to make a collective whole.

The mistakes that you make may not always be yours to learn, but meant for someone who is connected to you. Understanding these workings is what the human mind attempts to do. However, it is only necessary for you to except them and move on. Getting past your mistakes can be a large hurtle. To do so means that you must be painfully honest with your-self.

In turn, living in the future is also a fruitless endeavor. This is not to say that no one should ever worry about the future or what is to come. Rather, it simply means to not live or remain in this constant state. To do so would be denying oneself of life's greatest pleasures.

Spending your time making plans of adding riches to your coffer is only taking away from the richness of every moment that you have right now. It diminishes the joy you could be experiencing in the here and now. Concentrate on the here and now, because it is the only true time that we as humans, with a limited knowledge and understanding, have on this earth.

There are no metaphysical theories that you will have to learn in order to practice Zen Buddhism. It is just a simple matter of practice. Find a special place which will be your dojo, your room for contemplation where you can focus without interruptions.

You can begin by choosing a comfortable sitting position, and just relax. **Learn to let go.** It might be hard at first, because we are programmed to constantly think about everything: home, work, relationships, obligations, etc.

Our worries are always on our mind. Building up to create a collective disease in our minds that only eats away at our happiness. Learning how to let go will be covered in more detail in a later chapter.

Zen Buddhism asks you to stop thinking of them during medatation, to just let go during this time and free your mind of any constraints. The only thing you should think about and concentrate on is your breathing and your posture: only that and nothing else. Let the rhythm of your own breathing relax you, and make your conscious and unconscious mind disappear. Let them become one with everything, one with the universe. Once you've managed to do this, you've found Zen Buddhism.

Chapter 2: Beginners Questions and Answers to Buddhism

All beginners have questions. It is only natural to want to learn and understand something new. Not all questions can be answered in this book, but there are some common questions that can be covered. While Buddhism is itself a form of religion, Zen Buddhism is more a philosophy of life.

Is Zen Buddhism a religion?

As you will read further on, Zen Buddhism is not a religion. The word Zen comes from the Japanese version of the word **dhyana**, which is Sanskrit for meditation. It is a way of life, incorporating the very spirit of man within it.

Buddha isn't referred to as a god, demi-god or anything of the sort. He was mortal, a normal man who managed to reach a state of higher spiritual enlightenment and wanted to teach his devotees how to follow in his footsteps.

Do Zen Buddhists pray?

No, they don't pray, as there is no GOD at whom these prayers would be directed. Zen Buddhism is not about any God. It is not concerned with asking for something or speaking to a higher entity of any kind. Zen Buddhism is giving and taking of the minds power that exists in us all and finding a balance to help us reach Nirvana.

Do I have to quit my religion to become a Zen Buddhist?

Absolutely not! Zen Buddhism is beyond any religion, and it generally agrees with the moral teachings of most religions. So no, there is no need to quit any religion, as long as its teachings aren't in contrast with what Zen Buddhism teaches. Any religions that go against self-improvement, self-confidence, building self-esteem, or does not want its followers to be self-reliant would not fit well with the practice of Zen Buddhism.

What do I have to do to become a Zen Buddhist?

Practice Zazen, and be aware of the here and now. There is no special book to read, no scriptures to learn, no test to pass. There is no ceremonial event in which you must participate, nor is there any ritualized custom that you must go through to practice Zen Buddhism. It only calls for the willingness look within your-self.

What daily habits will I have to change to become a Zen Buddhist?

Zen Buddhism will not change any part of your essence that is doing you good. Your life will continue functioning as before, you will just feel a certain inner change, as you'll see yourself enjoying every moment to its fullest, you'll be able to concentrate on what is before you (and not what happened earlier on, or what will happen later), and most importantly, you will be in harmony with the world and people around you.

Where does Zen Buddhism stand on personal desires, namely sex, ambition, etc.?

As you will read in the following pages, Zen Buddhism doesn't teach complete suppressing of desires, as this is equally bad as giving in to them. What Buddha teaches is The Middle Path, I. e. learning how not to become slaves to our desires and the attachment to worldly possessions. In this sense, sex is just another aspect of the human nature.

Without it we wouldn't exist, so we should not suppress our need for it. However, balance is the key. One shouldn't engage in any sexual misconduct and not place too much attachment to it. The same applies to ambition: too much or too little, and you've become a slave to it. Reach a balance and you've got it.

Does Zen Buddhism teach reincarnation?

No. While Buddhism does embrace the concept of incarnation, Zen Buddhism is concerned with the here and now, not with what comes after. It emphasizes the idea that the human mind is unable to grasp deep spiritual truths that are concerned with the universe, so the only thing it can do is become one with it and use the moment it has to its fullest.

Chapter 3: Learning To Let Go

Medatation, when done right, can be an extremely enlightening experience. This chapter will cover the basics of what you will need to know to begin your path to a better you. The most important thing for anyone who is just beginning to learn how to meditate is to not expect great results, or an instantaneous breakthrough of mind blowing wisdom in the first few times.

It takes practice to learn how to medatae correctly. It can be exasperating for the beginner to learn. Do not give up simply because you could not achieve a state of medatation right away. This is very common for beginners.

Some people will find it easier to do than others. This is because those of us who have a deeper attachment to earthly things will find it harder to put them aside. Their minds stay in a constant active state to keep up with all their attachments.

Like the pond ripples, if only one stone hits the surface, it causes several ripples to go out, disturbing the natural state of tranquility. But, if several stones are thrown, there is caus.

The following steps will help you understand better the process of meditation. Keeping in mind that these steps are meant to help those who are learning.

Time

Picking the right time to meditate can be a very important factor in how successful you are. You will need to choose a time when outside factors will not interfere.

Take into consideration what mood or frame of mind that you are in. Being upset or angry are hard emotions for the beginner to overcome. It is best to begin with a calmer mindset.

The time of day you choose can make a difference as well. Because meditation requires a calmness of the body and mind, do not choose a time when either is feeling energized or over-active.

If you are worried that you may achieve a state of medation but how then will you come out? Set an alarm clock. Give yourself at least a couple of hours or more.

Place

You should take into consideration the place that you choose to meditate. Indoor or outdoor?

The temperature around you should be at a comfortable level. Too hot or too cold can hinder your mind from taking focus away from the body.

You need a place where there is nothing in your surroundings to offer distraction. When you are first learning, every small sound can become a distraction. Ticking clocks, computer humming, birds, insects, these can all become load nuisances when trying to stop the thinking process.

Body

Position- It is best to begin by taking a seated position. You can learn later how to meditate other ways. The seated position (for now) will allow you to take focus off the body's comfort.

Posture- Sitting with the correct posture is a must. As you learn to breathe correctly the posture of your body will insure a good blood flow. If one position does not feel comfortable to you, try another. You should not put your body in any position that causes pain.

Breathing- A slow, rhythmical breathing pattern is needed. You want to insure the body keeps a good supply of oxygen. Breathing too fast or too slow can change the amount of oxygen and carbon dioxide that your body exchanges. This fluctuation can affect your body and mind.

Mind

You must be in the right mindset before you begin your medatation time. If you are having trouble gaining calmness, don't start yet. Try doing something that will help your mind relax: take a bath, listen to music, read, anything that usually works well for you will do.

If you do not believe that you will gain anything from the experience of meditating, do not bother to try. A negative mindset will only insure that that is what you will receive, and you would only be wasting your time.

Let go

Now that the major considerations have been covered, and you feel that you are ready to learn to let go, make your preparations. When you have your time, place, body and mind ready to begin, it is time!

In your chosen place, take a seat on the floor (furniture is not advised due to the possible discomfort of prolonged sitting) and get into position. If a flat cushion helps, then by all means, use one. Cross your legs, straighten your spine, and neck into an in-line position.

Place both hands in your lap. You can lay them on your legs or lase your fingers, or lay on atop the other; it does not matter as long as your hands are open. Do not close them into fists as this impedes blood flow.

Set for a few minutes. There is no pressure to begin right away. Take notice of your surroundings, how your body is feeling, run through the events of your day. This time is to let your body get adjusted to the position and to let your mind wonder freely. Thinking about these things will allow your mind to let them go.

When you feel that you are relaxed and ready, you can begin.

Take a few slow, deep breathes, before closing your eyes. Keep your focus on your surroundings. The image in your mind beyond your closed lids. Concentrate on what you hear and feel. Until you are ready to let go of your surroundings and move deeper into your mind you will not get any farther then this step. Again, focusing on it will help your mind let it go.

Feel your feet, legs, butt, moving slowly up the body. Feel your stomach, spine, neck, and head. Notice how the brain feels. It is a part of your body, not you soul. They are two separate entities. Your brain works to keep the body functioning, but your mind is the thinker.

Breath

Return your focus to your breathing. Breathe with your mouth, not through your nasal cavities. It is a less restricted pathway. Slow, deep, rhythmical breaths.

This is the time that most beginners have the hardest with. Attempt to let go of everything except your breathing. Once this is accomplished, finally let go of that too. When you do, you may not even consciously know it. After all, you are attempting to reach your sub-conscious that is not concerned with your surroundings and its functions.

This state is the state of medatation. What happens during this time is a very spiritual experience for most. It is up to you what you wish to share with others about your experience. Although, because it is such an intensely personal experience, most people do not share it with others unless they feel that those whom they are sharing with can understand the experience.

Chapter 4: An Introduction to Buddhist Principles

The Four Noble Truths:

The story of The Four Noble Truths follows Buddha and the moment of his attainment of spiritual enlightenment. Having a great desire to share this moment with the rest of the world, he devised what is now commonly referred to as The Four Noble Truths.

Buddha, whose actual name was Prince Siddhartha, was confined within the palace walls by his father, who wanted to spare him the misery and heartache reigning outside the palace walls. But, Siddhartha was plagued by a curiosity to see reality. Once he was presented with this opportunity, he was shocked by what he witnessed. He was awed by the old and the sick, the poor, the feeble, and the dead. This bitter suffering left an immeasurable imprint on his young heart.

This unbiased exposure was what caused him to realize that everything that lives must suffer.

1. To live means to suffer.

Buddha realized through his awakening that all things living must suffer. Loved ones get sick and die. We get deprived of that which we desire the most, and even if we do obtain it, the satisfaction is all too short lived, and we are back where we started from. As humans, we are imperfect, and so is the world in which we live.

To fully know Autumn one must experience Winter. To fully know the rain one must experience the drought. Life would mean nothing without death, and love would mean nothing without loss. There must be a balance in all things.

2. The origin of suffering is attachment.

We all want something. It is in our blood. Desire reins our lives, and in turn, causes suffering. It is impossible for us humans to obtain every single thing that we crave. This leads to dissatisfaction, anxiety, anger and misery.

However, denying ourselves the desire it-self is equally bad. Denying our desires would be denying our-selves, denying life. So, neither of the two extremes is appropriate.

Rather, we need to teach ourselves how not to want too much, and so, we won't be forced to suffer unnecessarily. Because we do not suffer from a loss of things that we do not care about, our suffering only comes from the things that we are most attached to. It is good for us to be attached to certain people, but there should be no object in life that if lost, could cause us undue amounts of suffering.

3. Cessation of suffering is achievable.

As it was just mentioned, it is possible to diminish the amount of suffering we go through, if only we find the proper balance. We need to want less, and not get attached to things which don't deserve our attention and affection. Granted, it is achievable, but through meticulous and continuous practice. Achieving this state of mind, where we are released from worldly desires and in turn, released from worry, problems and suffering is achievement of the ultimate spiritual liberation, called "Nirvana."

4. The path to release from suffering.

It's all about finding our proper balance. By leading a balanced life that follows the Eightfold Path we will find our-self free from suffering. The perpetual path to self-improvement is not the easiest road, by no means, but it can be the most rewarding.

The Eightfold Path

The Eightfold Path is the path followed by a true Buddhist, in order to achieve Nirvana. These eight ideas are all intertwined, proving that the right state of mind not only leads to the right speech and actions, but also to the right way of life.

1. The Right View

   The right perspective is everything. Learn how to look at things without sugar-coating them. See objects, places and people around you for what they really are, and learn about the transience of all worldly things and possessions. In other words, try to look at things with an honest and open mind. Do not draw conclusions from what you first see.

2. The Right Thought

   The right perspective allows you the right thoughts, which are invaluable on your path to enlightenment. It has been scientifically proven that your thoughts guide your

24

actions, so why not make them right? The right kind of thoughts should focus on one's purpose in life and adhering to that purpose.

Because your thoughts are what guide you into action, make it a practice to think positively and try to avoid any negative thinking. Positive receives positive, while negative receives only more negative. Creating the right thoughts sets you on a harmonious path.

3. The Right Speech

The right speech is preceded by the right thoughts. Learn how to use words to your advantage, steer clear of too much idle chit-chat which doesn't have any depth. Speak the truth and refrain from offensive language that may cause you any negativity.

Your words should follow your thoughts, which should be focused on your life goal. Some people can find this harder to do than others, but once you are in sync with this process you will reap the many benefits. The key is to think before you speak.

4. The Right Action

Try leading a balanced life, while behaving peacefully and in harmony with others around you. You need to try to avoid unnecessary attachments, and abstain from any negative misconduct. Your actions can bring about other actions. Basically, it means to try to be a good and kind person.

Treating people well, no matter how you are treated, is always to right action. This is not the general mindset for the human race, but isn't relearning that mindset, to become a better, more enlightened person, why you are considering Zen Buddhism? Making the right action will bring you to a change.

5. The Right Livelihood

Do not spend your time and effort to gain wealth (whether monetary or of other possessions) by deceit. Anything gained in life should be received by an honest, trustworthy, and lawful manor. To do so only brings sorrow to your-self. Don't engage in unlawful businesses and earn your bread the right way.

6. The Right Effort

Work towards self-improvement, try to gain control over your thoughts and guide them in the right direction. Always be positive, don't harbor any ill will and forgive, rather than demand revenge, as it eats you up on the inside. Holding on to grievances is living in the past, and it only serves to build an infectious disease that will destroy any happiness that you attempt to build upon it.

Letting go of any ill will or jealousy can serve you better than harboring it. Do not let their negativity take root because it is very deep that you have to dig to uproot them. Replace all your negative thoughts and ideas with positive, optimistic ones and the change in your life will be instantaneous and astounding.

7. The Right Mindfulness

Focus on developing yourself spiritually, while trying to abstain from worldly distractions. Don't be led by greed, anger, and revenge. Rather, concentrate on your thoughts, emotions, and mental faculties. When you learn to let go of the earthly things you can free your spirit to grow and begin to comprehend enlightenment.

8. The Right Concentration

In order to reach spiritual enlightenment you must obtain the right concentration first. Be mindful of your thoughts, ideas, and actions. You must learn how to let go of unnecessary needs and desires that cause suffering and hold you back. Focus instead, all your mental capabilities on the current moment in order to achieve spiritual enlightenment.

The Middle Path

When Prince Siddhartha realized the truth of all the suffering in the world, he gave up all of the riches bestowed upon him by his royal descent, and turned to a life of abstinence. He refused all worldly machinations, and lived basically just to survive, which left his body on the brink of death. In doing this he realized that just like over-indulgence in the worldly desires and possessions, exaggerated abstinence was also not the right path to self-development and eventual enlightenment. They are both two extremes, and were unsuitable for his purposes.

He realized that in order to reach Nirvana he had to accept both and avoid both. In other words, he had to find the middle ground, or as he called it The Middle Path. Zen Buddhism is all about the unity, the oneness of the mind and the body. One must gain an understanding of how the material and spiritual components complement each other. This is why finding the right balance is stressed so often in this book.

The Three Jewels

While so many of us look for salvation and satisfaction from external sources, Zen Buddhism urges us to look for those same notions within ourselves. **We have to become our own shelter.** We have to find within ourselves the power we need.

The Three Jewels also referred to as The Three Refuges are: The Buddha (The Teacher), The Dharma (The Teaching) and The Sangha (The Buddhist Community).

This means that through taking refuge within these three ideas, one is learning how to realize one's own true nature. We must embrace our good along with our faults. Through commitment, resolve, harmony and focus, we can finally reach spiritual enlightenment.

While the saying, "People only treat you bad if you allow them to" may be true, the same goes for yourself. You cannot allow bad self-treatment. This is the behavior of self-destruction, and will only have one outcome.

Chapter 5: Beliefs That Buddhists Live By

Life is a subjective dream, where we are all actors in our very own, very special theatrical play. We know only as much as our lines allow us to know, no more, no less. Our life experiences make up the role that we play.

We know what the consequences for our actions would be. Still, we are left in awe before more profound questions such as the ones concerning life, death, the afterlife, etc. Our knowledge is limited, simply because it is the knowledge of a human.

Buddha Is Not a God

Buddha was a simple human man who found enlightenment and wanted to share it with others. He was not the first, nor the last, to find enlightenment, but he was a great teacher. He was able to teach his understandings in a way that it could be understood by many.

Buddhism itself is not a religion, but a philosophy, a way of thinking. It is not a matter of believing in any certain faith or rules as religion does. It pertains more to gaining the concept of self-awareness.

Living In the Here and Now

Zen Buddhism does not seek to answer these questions that have been plaguing mankind for centuries. For Zen Buddhism, they are secondary. The primary objective is seizing the here and now, letting go of what might or might not come afterwards.

Buddhism does teach that because of the universal connection of every living thing, all actions done or not done, in this life or in prior lives will be felt in the next one. As ripples in the water, our actions continue on. The teachings of Buddhism aim at opening our minds to seeing these effects and learning to escape from this endless cycle of our own making.

It does not offer confirmation, or a denial, of the incorporeal phenomena regarding a possible afterlife. It simply claims that humans, due to their limited conscious, are unable to understand or grasp the truth. Thus, all one can do is look for the truth within oneself by achieving oneness with the universe.

Some religions try and offer shelter outside oneself. They offer the answers to the questions 'why' and 'how'. But in reality, while faith can serve as a refuge, what then is a man who has lost his faith?

Believing in Oneself

Belief and conviction are strong suits of armor against most of the negative things in life. But, if that faith is broken and the teachings that were once depended upon become unreliable, people become lost. They have no solid ground on which to stand.

The human mind needs to gain strength from itself, not from any outside belief that could crumble and cripple it. One of the most intense sufferings that we as humans can bear is a loss of faith. It is not wise to rely upon any religion more than oneself.

We have to distinguish between illusion and reality; we must turn inward, towards our own spirituality. The Truth lies within us, not outside. Zen Buddhism doesn't give any answers, and this is where the core of its wisdom lies. True freedom lies within the teachings that show a man how to think, not what to think or what to believe in.

Universal Karma

Buddhists believe that with understanding and wisdom there is a natural desire for compassion.

True wisdom is not obtainable without compassion for those around you. Compassion itself helps us expand our knowledge and wisdom.

Buddhists believe in Karma because they have a profound understanding of how everything (being, object, and thought) is interconnected. Nothing happens that does not affect something else, nor does anything happen that does not have a cause and effect. With this thought in mind, it would only make since that good thoughts and deeds will reap the same.

Just as bad thoughts and deeds will bring more bad thoughts and deeds. Therefore, we must retrain ourselves to think in a positive, harmless, and peaceful manor

Meditation is Important

We cannot understand others if we cannot understand ourselves. Meditation can bring about a deeper knowledge of ourselves, and in turn, others. When we open our minds to the vast connectedness of all things we can begin to become enlightened as to the workings of how every thought and action we have effects our lives.

Meditation is meant to be a time for quite, piece, and solitude. A time of undertaking that should block out all worldly worries and thoughts to create a connection to the unknown. It is a chance to step out of your-self and see beyond your own needs and desires.

Chapter 6: A Few Common Buddhist Practices

There are a few common Buddhist practices which can aid you immensely on your path to enlightenment. You can choose to do as much or as little as you feel comfortable with. Again, there are no set laws that say what you should and shouldn't do.

Meditation

Meditation is a central part of Buddhism, and it represents a method of mental attentiveness which allows for spiritual freedom. While several variations exist, and they are present in all forms of Buddhism, the two main ones are Vipassana, representing insight, and Samatha, symbolizing tranquility.

- *Vipassana*; or insight meditation

This has an important goal of allowing you to reach essential, spiritual truths. When practicing Vipassana, one has to enter a trance-like state, where the object of focus is mindfulness. Once a person has mastered the sitting mindfulness, he can switch to walking mindfulness. This is practiced by monks in monasteries, as they manage to lose themselves in the simple activity of walking.

They achieve a state of "lack of self", where they are one with the world around them. Consequently, one can achieve a mindful presents in everyday activities, and the strength of living in the current moment is empowered to the extreme. This allows a person to participate more fully in whatever they are doing at the moment.

- *Samatha*, or tranquility meditation

This is the practice of teaching the mind how to concentrate better. In order to achieve the goal of Samatha meditation one has to detach from the world around him, while feeling happiness and tranquility. Then concentrate without the need to reason and explain. Then feel the happiness passing but holding on to the tranquility, until even the tranquility is gone. What is left is the goal of Samatha: composure and self-possession.

Mantras

According to Zen Buddhism, mantras are sounds believing to evoke god-like spirits. This will in turn awaken the supernatural powers that reside within the minds of men. They are also sometimes used as protection from evil and bad luck.

The most famous one is: "Om mani padme hum." While the meaning of these four words is vast, incorporating varied symbolic meaning, it is generally accepted (by the Western world) to evoke feelings and thoughts of wisdom. This causes the transformation of an impure mind and body into pure ones by following the path of Buddha.

Mudras

Buddhism uses mudras, which are hand gestures that symbolize certain sacred ideas and are usually presented through the image of a standing or sitting Buddha.

Also, there are prayer wheels which represent hollow cylinders with beautiful artwork mounted on a rod handle. They hold a wound scroll that has a mantra on it. Illiterate Buddhists can use it instead of actually reciting the mantra. Finally, there are numerous Buddhist symbols denoting Buddhist ideas, such as the lotus flower, the Bodhi tree, Buddha's footprints, etc.

Chapter 7: Zen Buddhism and It's Health Benefits

Zen Buddhism, particularly meditation and following the Buddhist practices can prove immensely beneficial not only for a person's psychological state, but for their physical state as well. Numerous studies have shown that meditation works wonders for the body and mind.

How Can Zen Buddhism Affect My Life?

Zen Buddhism has many health benefits that are both mentally and physically helpful.

- Reducing anxiety and stress

It helps you relax and have a better perspective on any problem which you might have, and in turn, a calm state of mind allows you to reach a better solution. Anxiety and stress can have an adverse effect on the body, causing a person to feel run down or tired.

- Better mood and behavior

Closely connected with a lower level of stress is the increase in positive mood and behavior.

Less stress immediately results in a better mood and general surge of happiness which allows you to fully enjoy life on an everyday basis. It has also helped numerous addicts get over their addictions, which according to Buddhism is simply an exaggerated form of attachment.

- Find a sense of purpose

Buddhism helps people with addictions find a sense of purpose in life; it fills the void of emptiness and allows for their mind to function properly once again. Even those who feel they have no goal in life can find a purpose.

- Regulates sleep

The meditation aids sleep irregularities, as sleep is detrimental to an overall state of well-being. The human body requires a certain amount of sleep to rejuvenate and create enough energy supply to carry the body through its waking hours. Without enough down time the body would not be able to keep up with the demands of the day.

- Builds up the immune system

It improves the proper functioning of the body's immune system through appropriate breathing and consequently, through a better blood flow. Both of these improvements can have a vital impact on the immune system. Everything in the body depends upon a healthy respiratory and circulatory system. The body's immune system can only function well if the others do.

- Improves your posture,

The human body suffers greatly in today's technology-ruled world. Many people find themselves slouching simply because their jobs require them to spend endless hours in front of the computer screen. Zen Buddhism can improve the posture greatly.

It will strengthen the back muscles when done properly. You will not only sit, stand, and walk properly with your head held up high, but you also won't suffer from back pain that is due to bad posture. Staying consistent with this practice can actually make your back pain disappear completely.

- More self-confidence

Better health leads to more self-confidence, and more self-confidence can lead to numerous other possibilities. Things that seemed beyond reach can feel attainable. The possibilities and benefits of Zen Buddhism on your overall state of well-being are endless.

You can see improvements such as a new and better job, a more compatible partner, a harmonious home, and a sharper mind.

There are no adverse benefits to practicing Zen Buddhism as a life philosophy.

Conclusion

This book covers just one small fragment of what Zen Buddhism really is. It is all a question of accepting these principles and beliefs, and incorporating these practices into your daily life. It is unquestionable that you will see improvement instantaneously.

You probably won't be able to reach Nirvana any time soon, but that's not the important thing. What really matters are the benefits that you reap along the way. Watch and enjoy as your life transforms from quick fast-forward flashes of work, family, eating and sleeping, into a happy, healthy life where you are the one pulling all the strings.

Take up meditation once a day and start with just a few minutes. Learn a few mantras and focus on how you pronounce them, discover what their true meaning is and how it can affect your life in a positive way.

Follow and uphold the Buddhist principles and never lose your way from The Eightfold path. Your thoughts are your words; your words are your actions; your actions are your life. Make sure they are the right ones.

Thank you again for downloading this book!

I hope this book was able to help you begin to understand what Zen Buddhism truly is and how it can help you embark on a happier and healthier life. The next step is to switch from words to actions and finally lead a life that you feel is worth living.

Finally, if you enjoyed this book, would you be kind enough to leave a review for it on Amazon? Your time would be greatly appreciated!

Thank you again!

Ashley Leesburg

Printed in Great Britain
by Amazon